photoFUN

Print Your Own Fabric for Quilts & Crafts

Hewlett-Packard Company ■ **Edited by Cyndy Lyle Rymer**

C&T PUBLISHING

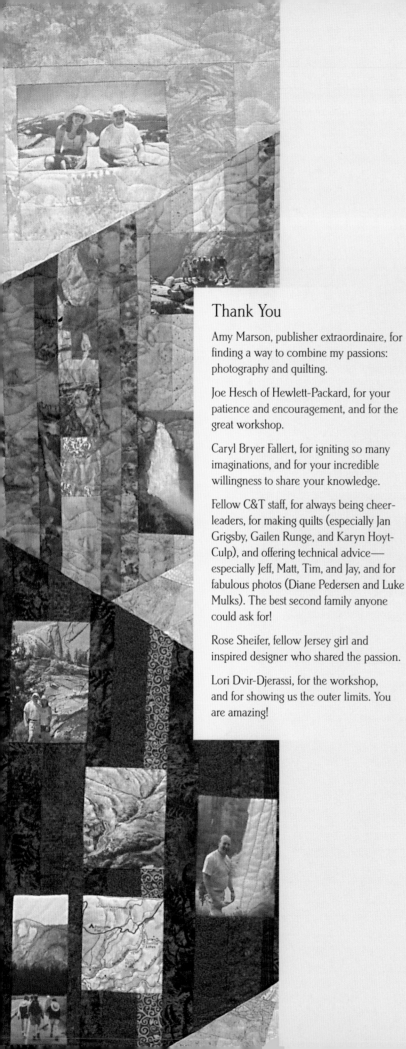

Thank You

Amy Marson, publisher extraordinaire, for finding a way to combine my passions: photography and quilting.

Joe Hesch of Hewlett-Packard, for your patience and encouragement, and for the great workshop.

Caryl Bryer Fallert, for igniting so many imaginations, and for your incredible willingness to share your knowledge.

Fellow C&T staff, for always being cheerleaders, for making quilts (especially Jan Grigsby, Gailen Runge, and Karyn Hoyt-Culp), and offering technical advice—especially Jeff, Matt, Tim, and Jay, and for fabulous photos (Diane Pedersen and Luke Mulks). The best second family anyone could ask for!

Rose Sheifer, fellow Jersey girl and inspired designer who shared the passion.

Lori Dvir-Djerassi, for the workshop, and for showing us the outer limits. You are amazing!

Text and Artwork © 2004 Hewlett Packard Company
Artwork © 2004 C&T Publishing

Publisher: Amy Marson
Editorial Director: Gailen Runge
Hewlett Packard Technical Director: Joe Hesch
Editor: Cyndy Lyle Rymer
Technical Editor: Sharon Page Ritchie
Proofreader: Eva Simoni Erb
Cover Designer: Kristen Yenche
Design Director/Book Designer: Rose Sheifer
Illustrator: Tim Manibusan
Production Assistant: Tim Manibusan
Quilt Photography: Sharon Risedorph, Luke Mulks, Kirstie McCormick, Hewlett-Packard Company
Additional photography by: Natalie Nakahara, page 5; Jan Grigsby, page 6; Rose Sheifer, page 13; Dick Thue, page 18; Adrianne Shroyer, page 28; K.C.Howland, page 30; Amy Marson, Lisa Loura, and Harry Jacobs, page 32; Joyce Becker and Cyndy Rymer, pager 33; Ed Betts, Scott Orloff, and Kirstie L. McCormick, page 47.
Published by C&T Publishing, Inc., P.O. Box 1456, Lafayette, California, 94549
Front cover: Hewlett Packard 2200 All-in-One shown with *Pet Owners' Quilt* (page 46), Cyndy Lyle Rymer, 2003
Back cover: *Family Tree Walhanging* (page 40), Cyndy Lyle Rymer, 2003

Library of Congress Cataloging-in-Publication Data

Photo fun : print your own fabric for quilts & crafts / Hewlett-Packard Company ; edited by Cyndy Lyle Rymer.
p. cm.
Includes index.
ISBN 1-57120-276-5 (paper trade)
1. Patchwork. 2. Photographs on cloth. 3. Transfer-printing. 4. Textile printing. I. Rymer, Cyndy Lyle. II. Hewlett-Packard Company.
TT835.P534 2004
746.46'0433--dc22
2004000236

Printed in China
9 8 7 6

Table of Contents

From Photo to Fabric

If Dr. Seuss had been a quilter, he might have said, "Oh, the quilts you can quilt!" Be forewarned: Making photo quilts, or quilts with your favorite artwork and other images, is addictive. While you work on one, you will come up with ideas for many more. HP inkjet printers make it easy to print photos and other images onto fabric. Now you don't have to search high and low for a copy shop that is willing to let you use their color copier to print photos onto photo transfer paper. A simple quilt project that features one fabulous photo—such as a pillow, potholder, or small quilt—can be made in about an hour. Scrapbook quilts with numerous photos, such as *Summer Memories* on page 50, can be made in a weekend.

It just gets more and more fun. Think outside the box a bit, and scan found objects such as flowers, leaves, or shells, and you can create your own yardage or borders. Create a small quilt that showcases one beautiful blossom in the center of a block. Make a family tree with many different photos of loved ones.

Are you about to run out of a favorite fabric that has been discontinued? Scan it to create additional yardage for your personal use, or play with the print to create an entirely new piece of fabric. Inexpensive photo image-editing software gives quilters the digital tools to create one-of-a-kind images. Best of all, the finished product is washable.

If you need to patch a worn spot on a favorite antique quilt, scan good portions of the quilt to create fabric for making repairs.

Quilters are incredibly creative people; follow the lead of this book, then take off in your own direction. So many possibilities! And just too much fun.

GREETINGS FROM

GLACIER BAY

Glacier Bay Memories, made and beaded by Mary Stori, author of *Beading Basics* from C&T Publishing.

Let the Photo Fun Begin

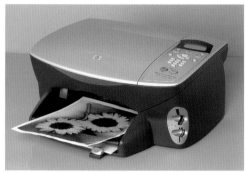

HP all-in-ones make printing on fabric easy.

How amazing to realize that you can quilt with just about anything: photos, artwork, clip art, memorabilia, birth certificates, scans of three-dimensional objects! All you need are an inkjet printer and pretreated fabric sheets. What's even more amazing is that you may not even need a computer. With the latest all-in-one machines, you can copy right onto fabric—without the use of a computer! The process is so simple: Plug the unit into the wall, push the copy button, make a couple of decisions with the options buttons, and your photo appears on a fabric sheet almost instantaneously. Best of all, the fabric is washable!

Fun Projects to Try

Here are a few ideas to get your wheels turning. Who doesn't have a closet full of old photos, or great refrigerator art provided by your favorite child or grandchild, that would be fabulous in a quilt?

1 Landscape quilts composed with a variety of your favorite flowers, sunsets, or parks visited

2 Pillows to give to friends to celebrate special times together

3 A new baby quilt with pictures of the proud parents, birth announcement, or the baby's brothers and sisters

4 Pet projects: Is there an animal in your life or a friend's who deserves a little recognition? Whether it's a dog, cat, hamster, or pot-bellied pig, you can make a quilted bed cover or pillow that features pictures of your favorite fuzzy friend.

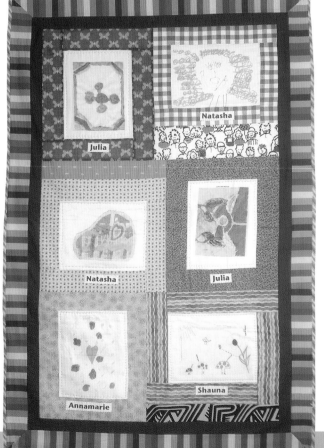

Refrigerator Art,
Hewlett-Packard Company

Tell a Story

Every picture tells a story, especially on a quilting project. You can use photos of anything to adorn your quilts—the possibilities are unlimited.

1 Scan pictures from your photo albums, boxes of slides, or negatives. Take photos with your digital camera, import them into your computer, and print them on fabric.

2 Print images from a photo CD made from your own conventional film, from your digital camera, or from a copyright-free collection of photos.

3 Download photos from copyright-free websites.

4 Use photos that have been sent to you through email.

Be sure you have the right to use the photos or images you choose. If you're the photographer, you own the copyright. There are lots of sources for copyright-free ("public domain") images (see Resources on page 63). There are also several companies that will license an image to you for a fee, sometimes a very small one. In most cases, you must get the permission of the photographer, artist, or designer to use a photograph, drawing, or fabric design.

Classic images, such as the Mona Lisa, are old enough to be in the public domain.

How quickly they grow into women!

How to
BUY A DIGITAL CAMERA

Do you need a digital camera to make quilts with photos? The quick answer is NO. However, digital cameras DO make printing directly onto fabric easier, and the quality of the photo printed on fabric may be sharper than with a conventional photo. By downloading images directly from a camera you are not printing a copy of a copy, you are printing an original photo. But as you can see in the quilts on pages 41 and 50, even very old prints work well when printed on fabric. Original artwork and three-dimensional objects also make wonderful prints on fabric.

Digital cameras feature memory cards that you can plug right into many inkjet printers and all-in-ones. With many HP inkjet printers, you select the photo you want to print, then hit COPY on the machine. That's it; magic! No computer necessary! In just a minute or so you have a photo ready to be sewn into a quilt.

Ready to invest in a digital camera? Here are some things to think about before you buy.

- Find a camera with a form of external memory storage such as memory cards. These tiny little things are the "film" for your camera. Again, the number is significant; the higher the number, the more photos you can store on the card. Memory cards with 128 to 256 megabytes (mb) will store a lot more photos than 32 or 64mb memory cards.

- Look for an AC adapter for your camera. This plugs into your camera, and into a wall socket. The best times to use the adapter are when you are transferring photos from your camera to your computer, or when you want to view your photos on the screen (LCD window) on the back of your camera. The adapter saves your battery power for the times when you don't want to be tied to an outlet, such as when you are actually taking photos.

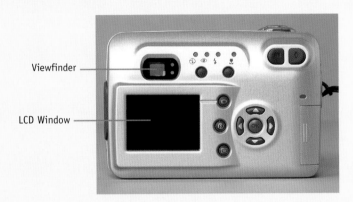

Viewfinder

LCD Window

BUYING A CAMERA

1.5 MEGAPIXEL
Around $100

File size for print on Best quality about 1 mb, suitable for email and viewing on the computer. Low-quality prints

1.5–3.5 MEGAPIXEL
$100–400

File size for print on Best quality about 3 mb, good for 4 x 6 prints and 3.5 megapixel provides suitable 8 x 10 photos

3.5–6.5 MEGAPIXEL
$400 to 2,000

File size for print on Best quality 3–20 mb, excellent 8 x 10 prints and suitable large prints from portions of the picture

6.5 AND UP
$$$$

File size LARGE, professional quality

- Make sure your new camera is compatible with your computer and/or printer. Check the type of connection ports your computer has, such as serial, USB, or IR. (Look through your computer documentation for this information.) HP printers accept almost all types of memory cards.

- Saving photos: Find a good back-up system for photos you want to keep. Saving photos only on the hard drive of your computer is risky: Think of how tragic it would be if your hard drive crashed and all of your precious photos were lost. Instead, think about backing up your photos on a writeable CD, which can hold up to about 15,000 photos!

- Still need more information? We know technology changes often, so to get the latest tips and information visit www.hp.com/go/quilting/book.

Heritage quilt, Hewlett-Packard Company

Before You Print

You really can print anything on fabric: photos, artwork, scanned images, and much more. Try using a decorative font in a word processing program to print a meaningful quotation, poem, wedding vows, or message for your project. Create one-of-a-kind fabric using your own artwork.

Photos look absolutely beautiful on silk, denim, cotton broadcloth, and so on. Smooth even weaves show the best detail in photos, but textured fabrics can create interesting effects, too. To order fabrics, check Resources on page 63. Photo wearables such as those shown at left are fun to make and wear!

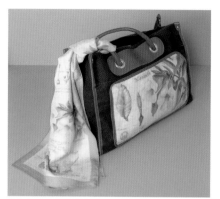

Original art is transformed into a scarf and purse. Created by Lori Dvir-Djerassi

Botanical prints by Wendy Hollander make a beautiful purse and scarf.

Reproduce the artwork on a plate to create placemats and napkins.

TIP

Got extra fabric? Just pretreat it with an ink fixative and experiment.

How to CHOOSE A PRINTER

To print on fabric, laser printers are not recommended.

Inkjet Printers

Inkjet printers are the most cost-effective, fastest, and easiest-to-use machines. Because inkjet printers spray ink to print, they are great for fabric printing. Hewlett Packard has a variety of inkjet printers to choose from, encompassing a wide price range and including many options for speed, print, and photo quality. You can find them at www.hp.com and other websites.

All-in-One Printer/Copiers

All-in-ones deliver multiple functions—printing, faxing, scanning, and copying—in one compact device. They make ideal candidates for quilters because they can do it all, and don't require a computer for simple printing. These workhorse printers are so versatile they have been referred to as the "Swiss Army" printer.

Newer all-in-ones make it so simple. Push the Copy button, and your picture is on fabric—without the use of a computer. Plus, the photo-quality output makes your pictures really shine.

FUN PROJECTS TO TRY

1 Feature one special photo, and use fabric, watercolor pencils, and quilting lines to extend the photo (see project on page 14).

2 Printed on fabric, photos are tangible reminders of the good times you had. Scan travel memorabilia like ticket stubs, receipts, unique containers, pictures, postcards, and hotel stationery to make a collage for a wallhanging.

3 Print embroidery or appliqué patterns on your fabric to make them easier to stitch or cut out.

4 Print photos on fabric for a photo pillow or wallhanging.

5 Create a windowpane quilt with a single picture printed in different sections (see project on page 55).

6 Imagine the impact of photos of four generations of women in your family, or a quilt containing images of parents or grandparents from their younger days (see project on page 50).

7 Don't forget to add a special label on the back of your quilt. Tell the story behind your inspiration. Put your picture on the label so future generations will know who made it. HP's Custom Label Kit gets you started (see www.hp.com/go/quilting/book).

If you have a digital camera, you can print pictures in a flash. On many new Hewlett Packard printers, you can insert the memory card from your digital camera and download pictures to your computer. Use the included software for basic image editing, like cropping and color adjustment.

The Proof Sheet feature is another reason all-in-ones are so easy to use. Push a button, and a proof sheet of all the photos that are on the memory card is printed on regular paper. Then choose the photo you want, and print it directly onto fabric.

You can even print pictures in different sizes, with multiple copies on one fabric sheet. Check the features of your image-editing software to create album pages or contact sheets. Always print a test sheet on normal paper before you print on fabric.

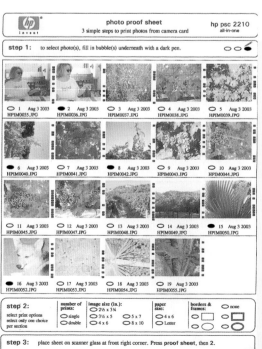

How to
MAKE YOUR FABRIC SHEETS FOR PRINTING

A fabric sheet is simply a piece of fabric bonded to paper. The paper stabilizes the fabric as it moves through the printer. You can make your own or buy them. Purchase fabric prepared for printing at your local craft or fabric store or online (see Resources on page 63).

Pretreated sheets cost more, but the quality is high and they are easy to use. Check Resources for ink fixatives to make your own fabric sheets. Most of the ready-made fabric sheets are pretreated with an ink fixative to make sure the printed fabric is colorfast and washable. Make sure the fabric sheets you're buying have been pretreated.

Supplies for making your own fabric sheets

Pretreated fabric sheets

What You Need

- Freezer paper, full-sheet adhesive labels, or other stabilizer
- Scissors or rotary cutter
- Ruler
- Cutting mat
- 100% cotton fabric (You can also try silk, rayon, or other fibers if appropriate for your project.)
- Ink fixative, such as Bubble Jet Set 2000
- Iron
- Lint brush

Prepare the Fabric

1 Pretreat the fabric with an ink fixative, following the manufacturer's directions for pretreating and drying the fabric.

2 Iron the fabric to remove wrinkles. Use a dry iron on the cotton setting for the best results.

3 Cut a 9" x 11½" piece of ironed fabric. By cutting the fabric slightly larger than the finished fabric sheet, you'll reduce the possibility of getting adhesive or plastic on your iron and ironing surface. You'll trim the fabric to fit the backing in a later step.

4 Use freezer paper, a full-sheet adhesive label, or purchased freezer paper sheets (see Resources, page 63) as the backing.

Freezer Paper

Here are some tips for using freezer paper to make printable fabric sheets.

1. Cut an 8½" x 11" piece of freezer paper.

2. Place the fabric face down on the ironing surface. Most ironing boards don't provide enough resistance to form a good bond when ironing the freezer paper to the fabric. Try using a cloth-covered table or piece of shelving.

3. Center the freezer paper, shiny side down, over the fabric.

4. Use a dry iron on a cotton setting. Start in the center and iron out to the edges until a bond forms.

5. Turn the sheet over and briefly iron the fabric side to remove any wrinkles.

6. Brush the fabric with a lint brush to remove any lint.

7. Trim the fabric sheet to 8½" x 11".

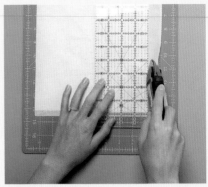
Trim the fabric sheet.

Adhesive Labels

Work with full-sheet labels; smaller labels (like address labels) may peel off and get stuck in the printer. Adhesive labels can be reused several times before they no longer stick to fabric.

1. Place the fabric face down on the ironing surface.

2. Peel the backing off the label. Line up one end of the label with the fabric, then carefully lay the adhesive side of the label on the fabric. Try not to get any wrinkles or bubbles under the label; a small roller, or brayer, is helpful to have on hand.

3. Flip the fabric face up and use a roller or cool iron to remove any wrinkles or air bubbles.

4. Trim your fabric sheet to match the adhesive label backing.

5. Brush the fabric with a lint brush to remove any lint.

Clip a small 45° corner off of the fabric sheet to prevent jams.

Before

After clipping corners

How to
PRINT ON FABRIC

4' banner sample being printed

First, here are some things you should know about printing on fabric.

1 Printers don't print white. If you're printing on colored fabric, the white parts of your image will be the same color as your fabric. And because the inks are transparent, the fabric color will affect the colors in your print. This could be fun; experiment! Something else to try: Print on subtle tone-on-tone fabric.

2 Remove all plain paper from the printer's paper tray. Insert one fabric sheet at a time to avoid jams. Check your manual to determine how to feed the fabric sheet into your printer.

3 The maximum width of your fabric sheet is limited by the width of your printer's paper tray, but you can vary the length by printing in banner mode. Refer to the Help file in your software application to learn how to prepare your image to print in banner mode (see page 9), and for the maximum length your printer can print.

4 The leading edge of the fabric should be securely bonded to the backing paper. If the fabric has separated from its backing, use masking tape or stitch around the top edge using a short stitch length.

5 Trim, don't pull, loose threads from the fabric sheet before inserting it into the printer. Loose threads can get caught in the printer.

6 Leave at least a ¼" seam allowance on all four sides of your image. If you print all the way to the edge of the fabric, you may end up cutting off some of the design. Keep in mind that some printers won't print all the way to the edge of the sheet.

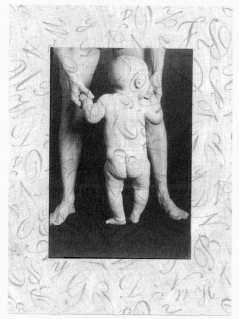

For a different (and fun) look, try printing on a subtle tone-on-tone fabric.

Print photos with space between them for seam allowances.

7 Don't use steam to press pretreated fabric sheets before printing—it may leave water spots on the fabric, or cause the fabric to separate from its paper backing.

8 Wrinkles and bubbles can create havoc and jams. Check your fabric sheet before printing to make sure it's smooth and wrinkle-free.

9 Print your image using the print settings that worked best on the plain paper.

10 Allow the ink to dry completely before removing the paper backing.

11 Follow the manufacturer's recommendation for setting and/or rinsing the fabric sheet before you start a project.

Here's that warning again: Print on paper first before printing on fabric.

Start with these general settings. If the colors that print aren't quite right, experiment with other print settings until you find the ones that work best with your inkjet printer.

Ready to Print? Here Goes!

- Open the file you want to print.
- Select **Print** from the **File** menu.
- Choose **Properties.**
- Under Print Quality, choose **Best.**
- For **Paper Type,** choose **Plain.**
- Click **OK** to accept the settings.
- Click **OK** to start printing.

Isn't that just incredible? Can you believe the quality of the print you are holding? Wasn't it easy? Congratulations! And now you can jump right into making a small quilt or pillow.

TIP

Save ink ($) and time by using the Fast option under Print or Copy Quality when you do your test print on paper.

Save your test prints! You can use them to lay out your quilt before you sew (see page 45).

TIP

Keep track of the settings you used for each test print by jotting down the changes you made right on the printout.

Single Photo Quilt

Cyndy Lyle Rymer,
Danville, CA, 2003

Finished Quilt Size: 15½" x 18"

Time It Takes to Make:
about 5 hours

Focus on just one great photo for a special smaller quilt. Extend the photo by adding fabrics that match the colors: light blue to the sky, beige to the sand and dunes. Watercolor pencils and free-motion quilting help enhance the elements in the photo, such as the dunes and ripples in the sand. It was fun to embellish this quilt with shells picked up from the same beach.

What You Need

- 1 pretreated fabric sheet
- Scraps of fabric to match areas of photo for borders and binding
- Backing: ½ yard
- Batting
- Watercolor pencils
- Threads to match

Photo Prep

Print the photo as an 8" x 10" photo, or use your scanner to enlarge and crop the photo, then print. Consider adding a caption to the photo prior to printing.

How to Make the Quilt

1 Peel the backing paper off of the photo print. If it proves difficult to remove, gently score the paper with a dull scissors. Add strips of fabric around the photo to match the colors in the photo. In this little quilt blue was added to extend the sky, and beige for the sand. Square up the quilt top.

2 Layer the quilt top, batting, and backing.

3 Stitch in-the-ditch around the photo to help it stand out.

4 Use watercolor pencils to add shading and color to areas that need some enhancement. Green was added to the sand to extend the tide pool.

5 Using a small darning foot on your sewing machine, and with the feed dogs down, add free-motion quilting. In this quilt, stitching extends the dune grass and ripples in the sand, and adds texture and depth.

6 Bind and embellish, if desired.

Friendship Pillow

Cyndy Lyle Rymer, Danville, CA, 2003

Finished Pillow Size:
any size will work

Time It Takes to Make:
about 6 hours

Adults should never lose a sense of playfulness, even after they become the mother of triplets, AND a fourth child, all under the age of four. Pillows are easy to make, and are wonderful gifts.

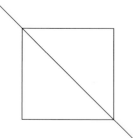

What You Need

- 1 pretreated fabric sheet
- ¼ yard each of 2 different fabrics
- ½ yard backing
- Pillow form

Half-square triangle construction

Photo Prep

Print the photo as an 8" x 10" photo, or use your scanner to enlarge and crop the photo, then print.

How to Make the Pillow

1 Peel the backing paper off of the photo print. If it proves difficult to remove, gently score the paper with a dull scissors or heat with a hair dryer.

2 If necessary, add a strip of fabric on all sides of the photo to make all measurements evenly divisible by a whole number to create the outside border of half-square triangles.

3 For 2" finished half-square triangles units, from the two fabrics cut 2 or more strips 2⅞" wide x the width of the fabric, then cut the strips into 2⅞" squares.

> **NOTE: If you need to make larger finished half-square triangles to fit the pillow top to your pillow size, just add ⅞" to the desired number (such as 3⅞" for 3" triangles or 4⅞" for 4" triangles), and cut strips, then squares, that wide. You can also add a second strip of fabric beyond the half-square triangle border to round out the measurement to the same size as the pillow form. (This makes the finished cover a little smaller than the pillow form, and the snug fit makes a plump, cushy pillow.)**

4 To make half-square triangle units, place 2 contrasting squares right sides together. Draw a diagonal line with a light pencil on the lighter fabric. Sew ¼" away from each side of the drawn line. Cut the squares on the drawn line.

Denim and piping were obvious choices for this small pillow.

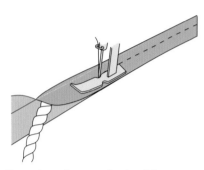

Use a zipper foot to make the piping.

5 Press the half-square triangle units open.

6 Sew the units together into rows, then add to the photo, sewing the strips to the top and bottom, then to the 2 sides.

7 Layer the pillow top with the backing, right sides together. Stitch ¼" from the edge, leaving an opening wide enough for the pillow form.

8 Turn right side out. Insert the pillow form. Slip stitch the opening closed.

Piping

Add piping around the edge of the pillow before sewing the front to the back.

Cut bias strips of fabric wide enough to wrap around your chosen cording, plus 1" for seam allowances. Seam the strips diagonally at the ends, if needed. Place the cording in the center of the wrong side of the bias strip, and fold the strip over the cord. Use a longer stitch and a zipper foot to sew the cording into the strip, stitching close to the cord.

With raw edges together, pin the piping to the edge of the pillow top. Sew to the top using a zipper foot, starting about 1½" from the beginning.

Stop stitching when you are about 1½" away from the first end of the cording and leave the needle in the fabric. Trim the second cording end so it will overlap the first end by about 1½". Pull out and trim ¾" of the cord from each end. With both ends extending into the seam allowance, cross the empty casing and finish stitching the cording to the pillow top.

Quilter's Lampshade and Pincushion

Sue Astroth, Concord, CA, 2003

Time It Takes to Make:
about 3 hours

A collection of vintage tape measures and buttons provided the inspiration for this lampshade and pincushion set that would look great in any sewing space. Scan the tape measures, then print as many times as needed to cover a purchased lampshade. You could also print spools of thread, sewing tools, and other sewing treasures.

What You Need

- Small lampshade; four-sided lampshades work well
- Tape measures, or other items to scan
- 4 pretreated fabric sheets
- Tacky glue, spray adhesive, or basting spray
- Ribbon

Photo Prep for the Lampshade

Arrange the tape measures or other items on the scanner bed. Scan and save at a size that will fit your lampshade. Print as many copies as needed on fabric sheets; 4 copies were required for this shade. Remember to test on paper first.

How to Make the Lampshade

1 Peel the backing paper off of the photo print. If the paper proves difficult to remove, gently score it with a dull scissors, or heat with a hair dryer.

2 Apply glue to the lampshade one side at a time.

3 Trim the fabric sheet as needed, and press onto lampshade, smoothing to remove bubbles. Repeat on all sides of the lampshade. Allow dry.

4 Cover seams with ribbon.

5 Glue ribbon to base and top of shade to finish, wrapping ribbon around the edge of the lampshade from front to back.

Pincushion

What You Need

- Pretreated fabric sheet
- Old buttons
- Scrap for backing fabric
- Crushed walnut shells—available at pet supply stores, or filling of your choice

Photo Prep for the Pincushion

Arrange a copyright-free print in the center of the scanner bed. Arrange old buttons around the print. Scan and save an image approximately 4" x 3".

How to Make the Pincushion

1 Peel the backing paper off of the photo print. If the paper proves difficult to remove, gently score it with a dull scissors. Trim the fabric sheet as necessary; allow for 1/4" seam allowances.

2 Layer the trimmed print and backing fabric with right sides together.

3 Turn right side out. Stitch, leaving one end open for stuffing.

4 Stuff with crushed walnut shells. (They keep pins sharp.)

5 Hand sew opening closed.

Capture the Image: A Guide to Scanning

One of the most powerful, flexible ways to capture images for printing onto fabric is to scan them. If you thought scanners were just computer add-ons, you're in for a pleasant surprise. With the help of these machines, you can add a whole new creative dimension to your photos, and to your quilts. If you don't own a scanner, your local copy shop will scan for you. HP sells quality scanners at low prices. Check www.hp.com to browse, shop, or learn more.

What to Scan

1 You can scan all kinds of photos—from antique pictures to panoramic vacation snapshots.

Photo by Dick Thue

2 Many scanners have optional attachments that let you scan slides, negatives, and transparencies. Get out that box of old slides and negatives gathering dust in your closet, and breathe new life into them by sewing the images into a quilt.

3 Scan three-dimensional objects like flowers, lace, leaves, or feathers to add a decorative touch to your project. Caryl Bryer Fallert's quilt on page 26 shows what can be done with a simple dandelion.

Scans of flowers

4 Memorabilia like old maps, letters, and advertisements offer an interesting, and often amusing, view of the past.

An old valentine makes a nostalgic heart-shaped wall-hanging that fits perfectly in a scrapbook cover.
Sue Astroth, Concord, CA, 2003

5 Scan the precious works of art hanging on the refrigerator, and preserve those finger-painted masterpieces.

6 If the shoe print is wonderful, clone it! Look at what can be done with photo image-editing software. The print on this shoe was scanned, then a rubber stamp or cloning tool was used to create fabric. The result is a matching scarf, and an old pair of jeans that was given new life as a skirt with a fabric insert.

Original artwork by Megan Richardson

COPYRIGHT WARNING: One thing to keep in mind when you scan: Many images are copyright protected. You should avoid scanning copyright-protected images.

Playtime, Hewlett-Packard Company

How to
CHOOSE A SCANNER

How to
SCAN

Following are the most common types of scanners.

FLATBED: A flatbed scanner looks something like a small copy machine, with a pane of glass where you place the item you want to scan.

ALL-IN-ONE: These machines are ideal for quilting. Flatbed scanning is only one function of all-in-ones; they can also print and copy without a computer.

SHEET-FED: Excellent for scanning large numbers of loose, individual sheets, but since they can't scan books or three-dimensional objects, they don't make an ideal scanner.

HANDHELD: Capable of scanning 2"–5" at a time, these are useful for scanning small images or passages of text, but not whole pages or objects.

A flatbed scanner or an all-in-one is the best bet for quilters, especially if you're interested in using scans of three-dimensional objects in your quilts.

Use a flatbed scanner to save a picture for a quilting project.

1 Place the artwork, object, or photo on the scanner glass.

2 Open your scanning software.

3 Choose at least 150 dpi.

4 Scan by selecting either Scan or Acquire from the File menu (or push the Scan button on the device itself). If you are using an all-in-one, you can scan and print directly on fabric, but you should print a test copy on paper first.

5 Save the image to your computer in either JPEG or TIFF format.

Photos saved at 50 and 300 dpi

Just What Is Resolution Anyway?

For good quality prints on fabrics, you need to be aware of resolution, which is measured in dpi, or "dots per inch." The more dots per inch, the sharper the picture. But the higher the dpi, the larger the file size will be.

Consider the resolution of your printer and the material you're printing on to determine the appropriate resolution for your image. If your printer only prints at 300 dpi, there's no point saving a big file at 1200 dpi, since the extra "information" just gets lost. And the tiny dots of ink spread a bit on fabric, so you can probably get a good print at a lower resolution than you'd use for a smooth photo paper. In fact, too many dots per inch on an absorbent fabric may bleed together, actually muddying or blurring the image. Test, test, test!

● Files scanned for email or the Internet should be 75 dpi so they send and load quickly, unless you're emailing them to someone who wants to use them in a printed project. In that case, scan and save the file at a higher (150 dpi) resolution. (If you need to send one or more large files, consider compressing them with a zip utility for the PC or StuffIt for Mac or PC before attaching them to your email.)

- A scanning resolution of 300 dpi works well for most text and images that are printed on paper.
- It's a good idea to first test different resolutions when scans will be printed on fabric. Scan and print a photo on paper first at 75, 150, and 300 dpi.

Lower-resolution images have jagged edges, especially visible in the detailed areas or in curved or diagonal lines. For most fabric-printing projects, a resolution of 150 dpi should work fine.

- Before scanning, decide what format you want to use to save the file. The two most common formats for image files are TIFF (.tif) and JPEG (.jpg).

TIFF files compress the image with no loss of detail, which is ideal for printing high-resolution pictures for a quilting project.

JPEG files are okay for pictures you want to use in quick image-placement projects (like a photo placemat or label). You do lose details each time the file is saved or re-saved, but JPEG creates smaller files. They're also good for posting on the Web or sending in email, since they're small and the loss of detail isn't crucial for low-resolution onscreen display.

Scanning Fabrics

Remember when Scarlett O'Hara used her drapes to make a new gown? Go one step further and scan your drapes to create lampshades, coasters, scraps, and more. It just takes pieces of fabric, creative project templates, and your imagination. Make sure you have a large enough piece left to get a clear scan. Remember fabric is copyrighted also.

Three-Dimensional Scanning

Think beyond paper when you are scanning images for a new quilt. There's a whole world of interesting textures, colors, and other artistic elements you can use in your quilts. Even paper looks more like a three-dimensional object if it's layered on other items.

Scanning Textures

For some unique textures try scanning household objects: plastic bottles, wooden spoons, crumpled aluminum foil, book spines, rubber bands, paper clips, shells—almost anything can look unusual or interesting once it has been scanned. Head outside for leaves, twigs, flowers, feathers, and plants to create natural images with real depth.

Mother Nature provides the most beautiful range of colors in fallen leaves.

Scanning Hand-Drawn Art

It's important to protect both the art and the scanning surface when you scan hand-drawn art. Be sure the artwork is completely dry before you scan it, and consider placing a protective transparency sheet on the scanner glass.

My Favorite Place, original collagraph by Kristy Konitzer

- **Art with crayons, markers, and watercolors:** Luckily, the type of art supplies kids are most likely to use are also the easiest to scan. For crayons, check the scanning glass afterwards and remove any wax flecks with a damp cloth.

- **Art with charcoal, pencil, and pastels:** Protect the drawing from smudges by spraying fixative on the artwork before scanning.

- **Oil or acrylic paintings:** If you have an oil painting with a pronounced texture, laying it down on the scanning surface may damage it. Consider taking a high-quality photo of it instead; this works well for any textured artwork.

Autumn Leaves Table Runner,
Hewlett-Packard Company

Playtime detail, Hewlett-Packard Company

QUICK PROJECT IDEAS

1 Scan a whole collage at once: Layer small items like coins and jewelry on the scanner glass, then place other items behind them like letters, the deed to a house, a map, and more, and use the collage as a centerpiece for a memory quilt.

2 Make your own fabric! An assortment of sewing notions or threads makes a meaningful print you can use to make small gifts for quilting friends, such as a pincushion for a quilt room (see page 17).

3 Make a four-seasons quilt (see page 51) that incorporates leaves and flowers from winter, spring, summer, and fall.

4 Create a collage of a wedding certificate, an engagement ring, pressed flowers, wedding bands, and a bridal veil for a special anniversary gift.

5 Quilt a scrapbook of your family history, with old photos, letters, stamped images, and heirlooms—even old maps and postcards can become a part of the picture (see page 50).

Scanning takes practice. Look around and think of all the things you can scan. Experiment with settings and controls to get the look you're after. Then discover another world of creativity at your fingertips.

Falling Leaves, Reynola Pakusich, Bellingham, WA, 2003. Scans of leaves printed on hand-dyed fabrics. For more information about circle quilts, see Reynola's book, *Circle Play,* available from C&T Publishing.

Repair an Antique Quilt

Restoring or salvaging an antique or damaged quilt may seem a little daunting. Where do you start? How can you find the right vintage fabrics to use? All you need are a scanner, an inkjet printer, some image-editing software, and a little practice.

How to
SCAN A QUILT

If areas of your quilt are stained, torn, or even missing, the first step is to map out which areas you want to repair or replace. You may want to draw a diagram on gridded paper to determine how much fabric is going to need restoration.

The next step is to find undamaged areas of the quilt that can be used to repair the damaged parts. Look at the fabrics used in the other blocks.

Carefully scan portions of the quilt; ask a friend to help you hold the quilt in place or support it on a table next to your scanner if you are working with a larger quilt.

1 Place the quilt face down on your scanner glass. Position it so the largest available piece of needed fabric is centered on the glass.

2 Scan the quilt using your scanning software. Use the cropping tool in your image-editing software to select the area that contains the fabric you need for repairing the quilt.

3 Save the image at a high resolution—at least 150 dpi.

Repeat these steps until you've scanned all the fabric samples you'll need to repair your quilt.

Don't worry if your fabric sample is only 2" square and you need for repairing a patch that's 3" long. You have a couple of options.

Make Color Adjustments

Solids: If the fabric is a solid color, you can use image-editing software to create a whole sheet of fabric that matches it.

1 Use the eyedropper tool to select the color you need.

2 Open a new image file, and choose the size you need.

3 Use the paint bucket tool to fill the whole file with the color.

4 Print the new file on paper and compare the color to the original. If necessary, adjust the hue, saturation, or brightness of the file to match it to the original fabric.

5 Choose a printable fabric that matches the feel or hand of your original as closely as possible.

6 Print the image on your fabric.

Clone and Copy

Print fabric: You may be able to clone, or copy, a printed fabric to make a larger piece.

If you simply increase the size of your image file to match the output you need, you will get a fabric with patterns that are larger than the original.

If you increase the image size by 200%, as shown in the following example, the flowers in the original fabric will appear to be twice as large when they are printed out.

1 Open your scanned picture in the image-editing software.

2 Increase the canvas size (not the image size) so the original fabric stays the same but the blank area around it increases.

3 If your software includes a rubber stamp or clone tool, use it to sample the original and paint in the blank areas. You may need to experiment with the brush sizes and settings before you are satisfied with the results. You could also try using the lasso tool to select individual motifs or irregularly shaped repeats.

4 If you don't have a clone tool, you can select the fabric swatch, copy it, and paste a copy next to the original. Use the eraser tool to remove any straight lines or visible edges; move the copy as needed to match the original repeat pattern.

Cloned fabric was used to create a brand new pattern using the same printed features.

Printing Cloned Fabric

Print the cloned images on a fabric that matches the hand and texture of the fabric you are repairing, matching the grain of the original fabric. Linen or cotton broadcloth may be good choices; see Resources, page 63.

Once you've printed your fabric patches, you can start repairing your quilt. Follow the manufacturer's instructions to set and rinse your printed fabrics thoroughly so the inks don't transfer to the quilt. Save your image files; this way, if you make a mistake, you can print out another sheet of fabric. (Before you start on Grandmother's damaged Log Cabin quilt, it might be a good idea to practice on a chewed-up old pillow first.) Handle fragile old textiles carefully; hand sewing may be more appropriate for repairs than machine sewing.

There is a world of options for scanning fabric. Look around, dig out those old photo albums, and imagine the myriad possibilities in scanning and quilting.

An entire ensemble was made by cloning part of a shoe. Lori Dvir-Djerassi, ColorTextiles, Las Vegas, NV

Dandelions in Bloom

Caryl Bryer Fallert, Oswego, IL, 2002

Finished Quilt Size: 28" x 28"

Caryl Bryer Fallert, Oswego, IL, 2002

Time It Takes to Make:
20 hours or more

Look what extraordinary things can be done with a common dandelion! A pioneer along the path connecting quilting and technology, Caryl has been experimenting with computers and photography for a while. In this quilt three different dandelion heads, including one gone to seed, and some dandelion greens were scanned and manipulated in image-editing software.

After saving the scans as TIFF files, Caryl enlarged the images to 8" square, then designed the blocks in CorelDraw. She added a black background to the dandelion greens in CorelDraw.

Caryl pretreated white cotton broadcloth with Bubble Jet Set to make the ink permanent, and printed the photos on her HP inkjet printer.

What You Need

- ½ yard white cotton broadcloth
- Bubble Jet Set 2000 ink fixative
- 1 yard backing fabric
- Border fabric: ⅔ yard
- Binding fabric: ⅓ yard
- Batting: 30" x 30" square
- Threads to match

How to Make the Quilt

1 Following the manufacturer's instructions, pretreat the cotton broadcloth with the Bubble Jet Set fixative. When dry, cut 6 rectangles 9" x 11½". Back with freezer paper or other stabilizer and trim to 8½" x 11" (see page 11). Alternatively, use pretreated fabric sheets.

2 Scan the objects for the center squares and sashing. Drape black fabric over the dandelions while scanning, or try leaving the lid open. Using your photo image-editing software, resize each center square image to 8". This includes a ¼" seam allowance on all sides, so do not crop too close to the edge of the flower or leaves. Print on the pretreated fabric sheets.

Caryl combined the sashing and corner square images using the software, and printed them on one sheet of fabric. Another option is to print them separately, and seam the two together. The measurements listed below are for the latter method.

3 Remove the paper backing, and trim the center squares to 8" x 8".

4 Cut 16 sashing strips 2½" x 8".

5 Cut 16 corner squares 2½" x 3".

6 Sew sashing strips to the top and bottom of the center square, making sure you sew ¼" in from the edge so none of the white margin around the photos shows.

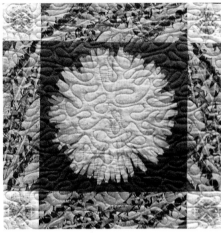

7 Sew corner squares to each end of the remaining sashing strips, and add to each side of the block.

8 Sew the blocks together into rows, then sew the rows together.

9 Add borders cut from 4"-wide strips.

10 Layer and baste the quilt top, batting, and backing.

11 Quilt in a meander stitch with yellow thread.

12 Bind.

A CD-ROM with all of the scans used to make Caryl's quilt is available at www.bryerpatch.com.

Take Your Best Shot: Using Photos

Using Photos in Quilts

You've probably had an idea for using pictures in your quilts for a long time. You ca[n] gather images from a number of sources: copyright-free photos downloa[ded] from a website, email from family and friends, or photos. Using HP hard[d]ware and software, this part of your project is now simple and fun to d[o]. But how do you get the most from your photos? This chapter will sho[w] you how. All you need are a few photos, an inkjet printer, and possibly a scanner if your photos are not already in digital form. You don't even need a computer to print a photo [on] fabric. You can use an HP all-in-one to copy a picture and print it multiple times.

How to CHOOSE PHOTOS FOR PROJECTS

1 Focus on one photo. Sometimes too many pictures can overwhelm a quilt project. It may be a good idea to use one picture as the focus, and if you bring in others, they can be smaller or less prominent.

2 Go for parallel composition. If you have five pictures that are head-and-shoulder portraits, and one that's a full-body shot taken from far away, it can be distracting. Try bringing the full-body photo into an image-editing program; resize it and crop the extra elements so it blends well with the other photos.

3 To use a photo in a quilted project, start with a digitized image, either scanned or taken directly from a digital camera. You can print it as is, or use image-editing software to improve it.

GOOD to KNOW

Image-Editing Software

All HP photo printers and digital cameras come with free image-editing software included with the device driver. HP photo printers can do many simple editing tasks such as color enhancement, brightness, contrast, cropping, and so on, right from the front panel; no computer is involved. Prices for retail software range from $60 to $600; the difference in price generally reflects the complexity of the software. Higher-end software packages have professional image-editing features that aren't necessary for most quilters. Ask around for opinions about the different programs, and try out one or two, if you can, before buying.

Image-editing software may have been packaged with your printer, computer, scanner, or digital camera. If not, Adobe Photoshop Elements 2 is a popular software choice, since it has many useful image-editing features. Other image-editing programs include PhotoDeluxe, Picture-it, PhotoImpact, and PaintShop Pro. These all feature tools that help fix the problems in your photos quickly, and are easy to use.

Open the File and Play

To get familiar with your image-editing program, open up a photo file and try out the tools.

Cropping: Use the cropping tool to select the part of the image you want to use. Edit out any extra, distracting areas such as the tree sticking out of the top of someone's head, or unwanted background clutter.

Uncropped photo

What a difference cropping makes!

Brightness/Contrast: Lighten up a dark photo with the brightness adjustments. If it is too light, you can darken it a bit. Most programs also have a feature that lets you adjust the overall contrast. If your picture is all middle tones (grays with no true blacks or whites), you can adjust the contrast to get a sharper picture.

Red-eye: Remove annoying red-eye in your photos with automatic red-eye removal, or with the pencil or fine paintbrush tool found in most photo image-editing software.

Image size: Change the size of the image to suit your quilting application. Remember that as you enlarge a small photo, the visual quality of the finished product generally degrades. By scanning at a high resolution or using the best quality setting on your digital camera, you can avoid images that appear grainy or pixilated.

Red eyes are easy to fix in most programs.

Restoring Photos

Pictures with stains, wrinkles, and holes may have character, but they can make your whole project look less than perfect. You can repair and restore cherished old photographs to their former glory, even if they're faded and discolored. These features are available in most imaging software programs.

Color correction

Quilters understand how important it is for colors to go together. But how do you match pictures from different decades? And how can you fix a photo that has yellowed with age?

Convert color to black and white: Use your image-editing software to change a color print to black and white. You can also do this simply by choosing "Print in Grayscale" on your print driver.

Sepia-tone pictures: If you want to match several pictures to use in one quilting project, a fast and fun option is to create a duotone version of each photo. Sepia tones are a popular choice for creating duotones of vintage photos; one color is black and the other is a warm brown, giving the pictures an antique look. This would be great for a vintage wallhanging, or in a quilt created with similar sepia tones (see page 50).

Fixing photo flaws

If there is a tear in the only picture of your grandfather, you can make it look almost new. Just be sure to save a copy of your picture as you go, so that if you can't undo what you've done, you have something to fall back on.

Most photo image-editing programs have a cloning or copying tool that allows you to take care of photo flaws by filling them in with similar colors from elsewhere in the picture. With heavy damage, the amount of work may look impossible at first, but just keep chipping away at it. The results are worth the effort.

Remember that you're working on an image that will, in most cases, be seen in a smaller size, in the context of a quilt, where small imperfections won't matter as much. If you don't manage to fix all the problem areas, don't worry. They'll add a little character to your picture.

Antique sepia photo

Black and white photo converted from color

Backgrounds: Erase or lighten the backgrounds to get a cleaner look.

Filters: Play with these to make your picture look painted or hand-drawn.

Text tool: Use this to insert words into your photo.

Original photo

Under painting filter

Neon

Save Your File

TIFF or JPEG? Save the file as a JPEG for pictures you want to use in quick image-placement projects like "made by" labels. See page 10 for more information.

QUICK PROJECT IDEAS

1 Make a photo window in your quilt. If your quilt pattern includes a house, train, boat, or building with windows, you can print pictures of friends and family and have them peeking out of each window.

2 Keep it simple: Turn one photo into a small postcard quilt that anyone would love to receive.

Postcard Quilt, Gailen Runge, Oakland, CA, 2003

3 Use a quilt design like Attic Window, and insert real landscape photos into each block. Learn how to make it look like a continous scene by creating a windowpane quilt, as described on page 55.

4 Make a living history quilt: someone in your family would love to receive a family tree wallhanging (page 40) or a quilted photo scrapbook.

Taylor's Memory Quilt, 92" x 106", Donna Blethen, Pacifica, CA, 2002. Details from **Matthew's Memory Quilt** below.

How to
TAKE GOOD PHOTOS

Since your photo memories will be a focal point of your project, you'll definitely want to make sure the snapshots are good. Here are some easy-to-learn tips that will give you a lifetime of better pictures.

Focus on Your Subject

- Fill the frame with your subject. Move in, or zoom in, until extraneous elements are gone. If these elements can't be avoided, crop them out later.

- Position your subject carefully. Point the camera at your subject, not at the background, whether it's your dog or a tropical sunset that you're trying to capture. Move as close as your camera will allow to your subject.

- Try to use pictures that have some visual elements in common so that they are appealing as a group, such as choosing all close-up pictures, rather than one close-up and a few from-a-distance shots.

Don't Say Cheese

Sometimes you want a perfectly posed picture (like a family portrait), but you don't need to pose subjects for every photo you take.

Try to capture life's moments as they are being lived. Say something to make them laugh. The pose will be relaxed and natural, allowing more personality to shine through.

Create an Appealing Composition

Compose your picture carefully. Do whatever you can to guide the gaze of the viewer to your subject.

Be bold; if your subjects aren't in the best position, rearrange them or move around until they are.

Nobody is using a stopwatch. Take time to move around and find the best viewpoint.

Hold Your Camera Steady

Camera movement is the most common cause of blurry pictures. Follow these steps to get the best photos.

1. Plant your feet firmly on the ground.

2. Steady your upper body by tucking your elbows in close to your sides.

3. Hold your camera firmly against your face.

4. Take a deep breath and gently squeeze down on the shutter release in one motion. Pressing down too hard on the button may cause the camera to jerk downward. Consider using a tripod, or try stabilizing yourself by leaning against a wall, car, tree, or another person.

Light It Right

Be aware of lighting conditions. Are shadows adding interest or are they distracting? Is your subject squinting? Using natural light rather than the auto-flash may set a better mood for the photo.

Avoid a Bull's-Eye Effect

Avoid placing your subject in the center of the photo. For greater visual interest, try to place the focal point away from the center—such as in the top-right or bottom-left area of the frame, for example.

Apply the "rule of thirds," a tried-and-true compositional technique. In your mind's eye, divide up the picture area into vertical and horizontal thirds (like a tic-tac-toe grid). Rather than placing your subject smack-dab in the center of the grid, try placing it on one of the two lines to create a picture with a more dramatic sense of scale or proportion.

Good composition

Layout Check with Test Prints

Print out your photos first on plain paper. Lay out the test prints to see how they work together: check for color, composition, and arrangement. Determine what size the pictures should be. This will save you time and money. Then on to the fun part: choosing or buying fabrics to use with your photos in a quilt or other project.

Labor of Love

All of your photo-filled quilt projects will benefit from your newfound expertise. But what really separates the best photo quilts from the rest is the affection and enthusiasm with which they're made. This patchwork of pictures and memories will be telling a story for many generations to come.

Tropical Vacation Quilt

Jeri Boe and Barbara Baker,
Bend, OR, 2003

Finished Quilt Size: 21½" x 18½"

Time It Takes to Make: about 6 hours

Enjoy a special vacation year round with this easy and fun-to-make wallhanging. This quilt would also make a special gift for your travel companion. So dig out those photos and put them on display. You're sure to smile every time you look at your wonderful creation.

NOTE: If the printed photographs are too small, sew on a strip of the background fabric to make them the correct size, or resize them in photo-editing software. Remember to leave a seam allowance.

What You Need

- 5-6 pretreated fabric sheets
- Multicolored print: ¼ yard for center
- Dark blue: ⅛ yard, cut into 1½"-wide strips for border 1
- Blue-green print: ¼ yard, cut into 2¾"-wide strips for border 2
- Binding: ¼ yard
- Backing: ⅝ yard
- Batting: 21" x 24"
- Clear nylon thread
- Rayon decorative thread

Photo Prep

Print your photos so they are the following unfinished sizes.

- 7½" x 5¾" for the center
- 1¾" x 2½"
- 3¼" x 2¼"
- 3¼" x 2½"
- 3¼" x 2¼"
- 3" x 3¼"
- 2¼" x 3¼"

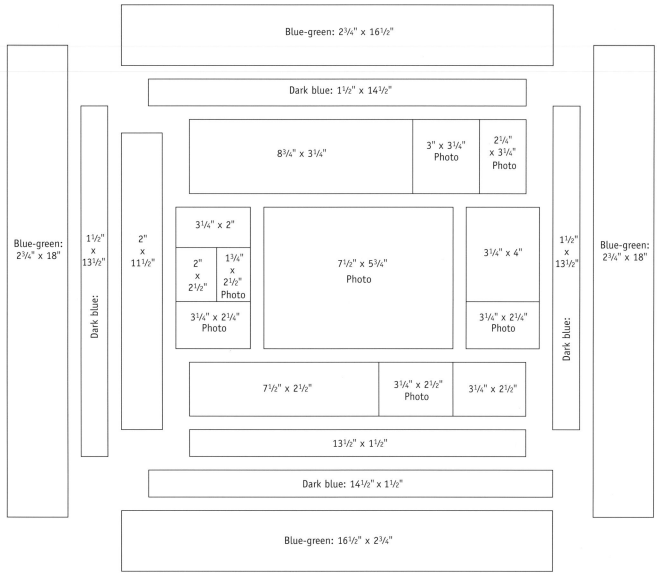

Blue-green: 2¾" x 16½"

Dark blue: 1½" x 14½"

8¾" x 3¼"

3" x 3¼"
Photo

2¼"
x 3¼"
Photo

Blue-green:
2¾" x 18"

1½"
x
13½"

Dark blue:

2"
x
11½"

3¼" x 2"

2"
x
2½"

1¾"
x
2½"
Photo

7½" x 5¾"
Photo

3¼" x 4"

1½"
x
13½"

Blue-green:
2¾" x 18"

Dark blue:

3¼" x 2¼"
Photo

3¼" x 2¼"
Photo

7½" x 2½"

3¼" x 2½"
Photo

3¼" x 2½"

13½" x 1½"

Dark blue: 14½" x 1½"

Blue-green: 16½" x 2¾"

Quilt Assembly Diagram. All sizes unfinished measurements

How to Make the Quilt

1 Follow the assembly diagram to cut and sew the strips as marked to the photos.

2 Layer the top, batting, and backing.

3 Quilt as desired. Use the clear nylon thread to quilt in the photos.

4 Bind, and attach a hanging sleeve as desired.

Wandering Around the Santa Cruz Mountains

Sandy Hart, Los Gatos, CA, 2002

Finished Quilt Size: 44" x 40"

Time It Takes to Make:
About 25 hours or more

For the more advanced quilter, this is a great way to use a number of wonderful photos. The quilt may look pieced, but the background photos are fused onto a backing of lightweight fusible interfacing. The Nine-Patch blocks in the borders were made with the same gradated fabrics in the rambling paper-pieced path, and beautifully tie the quilt together.

What You Need

- 15 pretreated fabric sheets (or fewer, depending on the number of photos you use)
- Fat quarters of gradated fabrics for path and borders
- Lightweight fusible interfacing: 2 yards
- Backing: 1¼ yards
- Batting: 46" x 42"
- Fusible bias tape, ¼" black: 3 yards
- Heavy interfacing
- Permanent black marker

Photo Prep

Start with a digital photo or scan your image. Resize all photos to 5½" x 5½" squares using image-editing software. Because of their size, you can print 2 photos on each 8½" x 11" fabric sheet.

How to Put It Together

1 Draw a grid on heavy interfacing with a permanent marker that indicates the number and the size of the photos you plan to use. Place a piece of lightweight, fusible interfacing cut slightly smaller than the finished size of the piece on top of this reference grid. Be sure the lightweight fusible interfacing is **fusible** *side up!*

2 The arcs: The winding trail consists of a series of arcs. Enlarge the pattern at right and paper piece 41 arcs.

3 Cut the arc(s) out of each photo before you place the photo in its correct location on the lightweight fusible foundation.

4 Place the photos and arcs on the fusible interfacing, using the reference grid as a guide. Be sure that their edges just touch. Gaps are not your friend.

5 Press everything in place on the fusible interfacing, being careful not to move the pieces around or to touch exposed fusible interfacing with the iron.

6 Vertical seams: Fold column 1 over column 2 so the background fabrics and arcs are right sides together. Sew ¼" through the 2 layers of fabric and 2 layers of fusible interfacing. Continue until all of the columns of blocks are sewn to their neighbors. Slit the interfacing seam allowances and press these seams open from the back.

7 Horizontal seams: Fold row 1 over row 2 so the background photos and arcs are right sides together and the vertical seams are lined up. Sew a ¼" seam through the 2 layers of fabric and 2 layers of fusible interfacing. Continue until all of the rows of blocks are sewn to their neighbors. Slit the seam allowances of the fusible interfacing and press these seams open from the back.

8 Cover the intersections between the arcs and background photos using a continuous piece of ¼" bias. Be sure to center the bias over the intersection and work it gently around tight spots and curves so it does not stretch.

9 Smooth the bias in place with an iron, centering it on the intersection between the pieces. If you have to reposition the bias to cover a raw edge, warm it first to avoid fraying the fabric underneath or separating the fusible strip from the bias when you pull the strip off.

10 Sew the bias strips along each edge to permanently attach them. Sew the bias down so that your stitching line is 1 or 2 threads from each edge.

11 Add whatever borders you desire, then layer, quilt, and bind.

Cover the project with a Teflon pressing cloth.

NOTE: The bias will thin to the point that it won't cover the edges of your fabric if you pull on it too hard.

Be careful not to quilt unevenly or too heavily; the quilted fabric areas will shrink but the bias will not, so the fabric may pull out from beneath the bias or your finished piece may not lie flat.

If you happen to quilt over the black bias with the machine by accident, cover the offending stitch with the tip of a permanent (Sharpie) black pen and nobody will be the wiser.

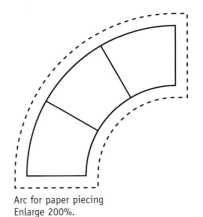

Arc for paper piecing
Enlarge 200%.

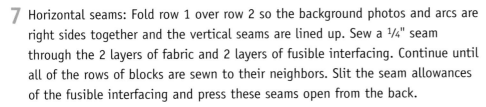

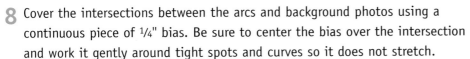

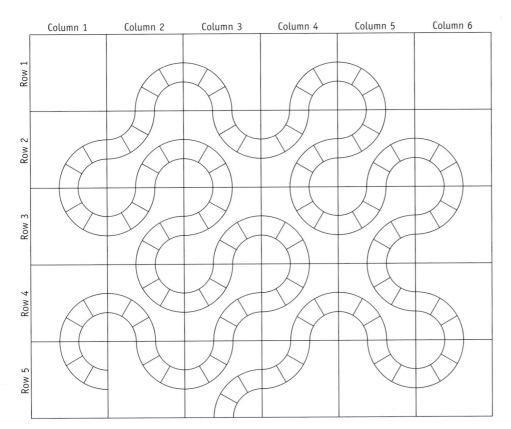

Quilting a Photo Memory

Signature or Memory Quilts

Photo memory quilts are the perfect way to tell life stories in living colors. Signature or memory quilts have been around for more than 100 years, and were very popular with Victorian quilters. These keepsake quilts are traditionally given by families and friends to commemorate birthdays, anniversaries, weddings, new babies, or to say goodbye.

A memory quilt might contain the signatures of loved ones, a significant quotation, and scraps of meaningful fabrics, from a baby's blanket, a favorite dress, or wedding textiles. Memory quilts tell a story or celebrate a special event in appliquéd pictures or words.

Printing on fabric has made it easy to create memory quilts that feature photos and other artwork. It also means you can make multiple copies of a single project. As every quilt artist knows, once you've made an amazing quilt full of memories for one member of the family, everyone wants one.

Technology has made it easy to include items on a quilt that previously were impossible to capture. Scanning baby toys or grandma's wedding ring and printing them to be part of the quilt is a fabulous embellishment and a way to capture memories.

With a scanner or digital camera and a printer, you can scan or take a photo of a scrap of fabric and print as many copies as you need for one—or 100—quilt projects.

You've probably planned to create a memory quilt for someone special for a long time. Whatever the occasion, here are ways to get started.

The Wedding Dress Quilt, 44" x 53", Reynola Pakusich, Bellingham, WA. Twelve photos of ten brides—four generations—who wore the same dress spanning the years 1910–1989! The original dress was made by Sara Little Reynolds, Reynola's grandmother, in 1910 of China silk ordered from the Sears Roebuck catalog.

Gather photos, artwork, memorabilia, and other special items from family and friends. Consider using everything from baby's first footprint to grandmother's reading glasses.

Search out other memory quilt material from sources such as your local library or courthouse, antique stores, or your grandma's attic. Interview older relatives to record their precious memories; bring a tape recorder so you also have an audio memory, and so you don't miss a single important detail.

Add a meaningful quotation, a poem, or a caption about the subject of the quilt. Use the HP Custom Quilt Label Kit to make this task easy and quick. For a special effect, the text can be faded and saved using image-editing software as one layer, and combined with a photo(s) saved as a second layer.

Choose the colors, fabric, photos, and heirlooms for your project and group them together to see how well they mesh. Tack the various elements to a piece of poster or foam board and view them from a distance. What are the dominant color themes? These are the ones you should consider using in your project.

Once you've created a memory quilt, don't forget to make a customized "made by" label that tells the story. You can also include a picture of your inspiration on the label.

Scanning Your Memories

Some things to consider: Which items will be scanned and printed on fabric and which will actually be incorporated into the quilted project? If you use fabric from your grandmother's dress, scan it first so you can save it as an electronic file to use again in other projects.

As you scan your pictures and objects, keep the color palette in mind. You may want to adjust the colors of your photos and memorabilia so they all fall in the range of the colors in your quilted project.

If you've never scanned before, review the basics of scanning on page 20 before you begin, and read about restoring vintage photos for tips on fixing flaws in your antique pictures.

FUN PROJECTS TO TRY

1 Make a genealogy chart that includes fabrics donated from each family member.

2 Build a circle of life with a photo of your family in the center, your grandparents and their families in a circle around you, and other relatives around the edges.

3 Create a wallhanging of your ancestors, then put together a matching scrapbook with the family history for everyone to read and enjoy.

Created November 2003
Cyndy Lyle Rymer
Danville, CA

Dear Kevin, Zack, and Zana,

We have such wonderful people in our lives, and I wanted to celebrate the family members you have known as well as those who came before you.

Did you know my grandfather, William Brown, started Brown Chemical Company during the Depression? And that for a long time Nana and my Uncle Art ran the business together before passing it on to the next generation?

Remember me telling you that Nana's mother's sister had a monkey for a pet? Look for the picture in the quilt.

Text printed on fabric for **Family Tree Wallhanging** (next page)

Family Tree Wallhanging

Cyndy Lyle Rymer, Danville, CA, 2003

Finished Quilt Size: 49" x 53"

Time It Takes to Make:
about 65 hours (or less, depending
on size and number of leaves)

A cache of old family photos unearthed during a family reunion inspired this quilt. Create your own collaged fabric for the tree trunk and branches, or use one special purple fabric. Bias binding around the outside edges of some leaves conceals floral wire, which makes them bendable, adding a three-dimensional look to the quilt. Just add leaves as your family grows. It's fun to include family pets under the tree. Consider printing a brief family history as a label on the back of the quilt; include a "Who's Who" for the leaves so future generations don't have to guess the identity of each relative.

What You Need

- 4–10 pretreated fabric sheets
- Greens: Scraps to total 1½ yards for binding and backing for 3-D leaves
- Purple: 1 yard for tree trunk, or scraps of purple for tree trunk to total 1 yard
- Light green: 1½ yards for background
- Light purple: 1 yard for inner border
- Multicolored print: 1½ yards for outer borders and binding
- ½ yard purple tulle
- Backing: 2 yards

- Batting: 53" x 57"
- Fusible adhesive web: 2–3 yards (amount depends on number of leaves made)
- Tear-away stabilizer: 3 yards, or use freezer paper
- Water-soluble stabilizer: 2 packages
- Yarns and decorative thread for embellishing the tree trunk
- Decorative threads
- Invisible nylon thread
- Wrapped floral wire
- Freezer paper

Photo Prep

1 Scan the photos you are planning to use (unless they are already digital images). Use image-editing software to resize the images so they are similar in size.

2 For printing, similar-sized photos can be grouped together using the album or contact sheet feature in your image-editing software. Be sure to leave at least ½" between the photos. Print on pretreated fabric sheets. Note that printing old photos in color rather than black and white retains the warm brown tones. If you prefer to have all photos in black and white, convert the files to black and white using your image-editing software.

Three-Dimensional Leaf Assembly

Note that not all of the leaves need to be 3-D; most can be fused to the background fabric. See Simple Leaves, page 42.

1 Following the manufacturer's instructions, fuse webbing to the wrong side of some scraps of green for the back of the 3-D leaves.

2 Remove the paper from the back of the photo sheets. Fuse webbing to the back.

3 Cut the photos apart. Fuse the photos to different pieces of green fabric. Freehand cut the layered photos into leaf shapes.

4 Cut 1½"-wide x 12" strips of bias binding from a variety of green scraps. Fold in half lengthwise to create short pieces of bias binding to go around the edge of the leaves.

5 Pin bias binding to one outside edge of the leaves you choose to be 3-D, aligning the raw edge of the binding with the edge of the leaf shape. Use a wider stitch to baste close to the folded edge of the bias strip.

6 Insert a piece of floral wire into the binding that is approximately 2" longer than the side of the leaf. Tug it toward the basting and pin. Use a wide zigzag stitch to sew over the wire in the bias binding. Be sure you are stitching over the wire as you sew, being careful not to hit the wire with the needle.

7 Repeat steps 5 and 6 for the other leaf edge.

8 Trim the wire at the top of the leaf; twist the bottom wires together and trim to a length of about 1"–1½". Starting at the bottom of the right side, satin stitch over the wire using a wider-width stitch. Next trim the outside edges of the leaf even with the satin stitching. Satin stitch the edge one more time for a clean edge. Set leaves aside.

Sew binding strip, insert wire, and pin.

Satin stitch over the wire.

Finish both sides of leaf.

Simple Leaves

1 Fuse adhesive web to the back of each photo before trimming into leaf shapes.

2 Cut each photo into a leaf, making a variety of leaf shapes and sizes. Set aside.

Collaged Fabric for Tree Trunk and Branches

If you have never experimented with making your own fabric from bits and pieces of fabric scraps and embellishing yarns and threads, you are in for a treat. You will need approximately 3 pieces 10" x 15" of collaged fabric for the tree trunk and branches.

1 Cut or tear strips of different purple fabrics in different values from lights to darks in varying widths, but at least 15" long.

2 Cut a piece of the water-soluble stabilizer about 10" x 30". Fold in half, then place on top of a piece of purple tulle slightly larger than the stabilizer. This helps the stabilizer glide over the bed of your machine while you are stitching.

3 Open fold, and randomly place purple fabric strips on top of one half of the water-soluble stabilizer so it is covered. Top with strands of embellishing yarns, silk ribbon, or whatever you have available.

4 Fold the other half of the water-soluble stabilizer over the top of the strips and yarns.

5 Drop the feed dogs on your machine, and use a darning foot. Grab hold of the edges of the water-soluble stabilizer sandwich, and free-motion stitch in long random lines over the layers. Change threads often, using a variety of different purple threads. Stitch until the stitching lines hold the scraps and threads together.

6 Rinse the layers under water to remove the water-soluble stabilizer. Allow to dry.

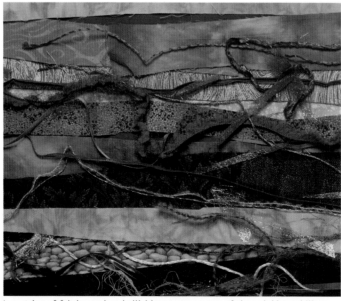

Lay strips of fabrics and embellishing yarns on top of the soluble stabilizer.

Finished collaged fabric

How to Make the Quilt

1 Cut a rectangle approximately 38" x 42" for the background. Back with tear-away stabilizer.

2 Lightly trace the outline of the tree on the backing fabric using a lightbox or window.

3 Trace the tree trunk onto the paper side of freezer paper to create a template. Cut out.

4 Back the collaged fabric with fusible web.

5 Using a hot dry iron, press the freezer-paper template for the tree trunk to the top of the collaged fabric. Cut out, remove the paper on the fusible web, and place on the background fabric.

6 Use freezer paper to create templates for the larger branches. Cut out, remove paper backing, and place branches on the background.

7 Free hand cut narrower branches and place on the background. Some of the narrower branches can be created with a satin stitch.

8 For the top thread, use nylon invisible thread, and thread to match the background in the bobbin. Using a narrow zigzag stitch, stitch around all of the edges of the tree trunk and branches to appliqué them in place.

9 Arrange the leaves on the background rectangle. Pin in place.

10 Satin stitch around the outer edges of the simple leaves.

11 Use a narrow satin stitch to create "branches" that cover the wires and attach the 3-D leaves to the tree trunk.

12 Layer the quilt top, batting, and backing. Baste.

13 Quilt around the tree, branches, and leaves.

14 Add embellishments as desired. Couching yarns were used to create the chains for the swing.

15 Bind. Add a hanging sleeve.

16 Create a story label that indicates Who's Who on the quilt top.

Tree pattern

Camping Memories Quilt

Cyndy Lyle Rymer, Danville, CA, 2003

Finished Quilt Size: 47" x 25"

Time It Takes to Make:
about 20 hours

Days spent fishing, swimming, and playing with cousins; nights spent stargazing and gorging on the fish caught and marshmallows over the fire—is there anything more special for an extended family? The memories can last a lot longer if you celebrate the time spent together by making a wallhanging that can circulate between homes throughout the year.

What You Need

- 3–4 pretreated fabric sheets
- Multicolored stripe or print: ¼ yard for photo borders
- Navy (or other tent color): 2 yards for tent and backing
- Light blue: ½ yard for sky
- Multicolored print: ⅛ yard for bottom border
- Print: 1 yard for outer border and binding
- Batting: 49" x 27"
- Permanent pen
- Optional: embellishments like fishing poles, fish, letters, leaves

Photo Prep

1 Scan the photos you are planning to use (unless they are already digital images). Use image-editing software to resize the images so they are similar in size. Make test prints on paper before you print on fabric.

2 For printing, similar-sized photos can be grouped together using the album or contact sheet feature in your image-editing software. Be sure to leave at least ½" between the photos for seam allowances. Print on pretreated fabric sheets.

How to Make the Quilt

1. Cut a piece of freezer paper to the approximate size your quilt will be.

2. Cut apart your test prints, and play with them on the freezer paper until you are satisfied with the arrangement. Use the permanent pen to mark off sections of the quilt: the tent and placement of all photos. Use the sections marked as templates.

Freezer paper pattern

3. Cut strips about 1" wide from the multicolored stripe or print. Sew strips on all sides of each photo.

4. Cut the freezer paper pattern apart into sections. Add strips or larger scraps of fabric to each photo to create each section; remember to add a 1/4" seam allowance to all sections.

5. Sew sections together.

6. Add bottom inner border.

7. Add side outer borders, then top and bottom outer borders.

8. Layer backing, batting, and completed quilt top.

9. Stitch in-the-ditch around the photos. Quilt 1/4" from seamlines. Finish by quilting other elements as desired.

10. Bind and add a hanging sleeve.

11. Glue or hand sew embellishments onto quilt.

Pet Owner's Quilt

Cyndy Lyle Rymer, Danville, CA, 2003

Finished Quilt Size:
28½" x 34½"

Time It Takes to Make:
about 12 hours

When you have many family or pet photos to work with, consider making one great photo the focal point, and add same-size smaller photos on all sides. This quilt was easy to make once all the photos were scanned and resized to the same size. Ganging the photos into contact sheets made it less expensive to print them out on fabric sheets.

Feel free to change the background and accent colors to complement your photos.

What You Need

- 4–8 pretreated fabric sheets (6 photos 2½" x 2½" can fit on one sheet)
- Blue: Scraps to total ½ yard for narrow sashing around photos (blue) and inner border
- Gold: ½ yard background
- Backing: ¾ yard
- Binding: ¼ yard
- Batting: 30" x 36"

Photo Prep

1 Print the center photo as an 8" x 10" photo, or use your scanner to enlarge and crop the photo, then print.

2 Scan the photos to use around the center image, and resize to suit your needs. Group them in album or contact sheets using your image-editing software. Be sure to leave at least ½" between photos for seam allowance. Print the contact sheets.

How to Make the Quilt

1 Peel off the backing paper.

2 Fold narrow strips (about 1") in half lengthwise, and tack to the top and bottom, then sides, of each photo, raw edges aligned, forming a finished-edge frame.

3 Arrange the photos on your design wall. When you are happy with the results, sew background strips between the photos.

> **NOTE: This quilt was constructed with 2 horizontal rows of 5 photos at the top and 1 row at the bottom. Vertical background strips were sewn between the photos to create the rows.**
>
> **The vertical rows of 4 photos were sewn together with horizontal sashing strips.**

4 Add borders around the center photo.

5 Sew the side vertical rows to the center photo, then the top and bottom rows.

6 Add a narrow inner border (about ¾") on all sides of the quilt top.

7 Add a wider border (about 3¾") on all sides of the quilt top.

8 Layer the quilt top, batting, and backing.

9 Stitch in-the-ditch around the photos.

10 One quilting suggestion for the outer border is to quilt words that remind you of your subject matter.

11 Bind.

Party Animals, 30" x 30"
Cyndy Lyle Rymer, 2003.
Apparently, the night of C&T's 20th Anniversary party, the staffers' pets got together and held their own party.

Scrapbook Quilts

Like quilting, scrapbooking is all about capturing memories. When quilting and scrapbooking combine, magic happens. Instead of a book, your pictures appear in a quilt. Scrapbook quilts can be made of fabric, or a combination of fabric and paper.

Plan your scrapbook quilt in advance, or just sew as you go. Print digital images directly on fabric, or make color copies of photos and mementos and layer them onto cardstock that is stitched onto the quilt.

You'll need digital photos, an inkjet printer or all-in-one that can print on fabric, and printable fabric sheets. It's also helpful to have a scanner and a computer with image-editing software so you can edit your scans and photos. Digital cameras make the task that much easier. Skip past scanning and use the pictures from your camera.

If you're copying your pictures onto iron-on transfers, you'll need HP transfer paper and a color copier such as an HP all-in-one.

Be All That You Can Be, 54" x 48", Sue Astroth, Concord, CA, 2003. Antique postcards are a great source for unusual images. Sue, author of **Scrapbook Quilts** (see Resources, page 63), combined a wonderful selection of scrapbook embellishments with photos.

FUN PROJECT IDEAS

This old house: Show before-and-after renovation pictures, scans of wallpaper, and include pictures of the family peeking out of windows.

A trip to the zoo: Use pictures of animals, scans of brochures, and animal-themed fabrics to make a photo collage.

Coming of age: Create a quilt to celebrate the milestones in a young person's life: a first communion, graduation, quinceañeras, or a bat or bar mitzvah.

Historic events: Make a quilt to show a timeline of history. If you saw the first moon landing or the fall of the Berlin Wall, use the pictures and scans of newspaper clippings to commemorate the date.

What a sport: Gather uniforms, team photos, scans of plaques, trophies, gloves, and balls to create a celebration of the athlete in your life.

Vacation: Gather photos, souvenirs, and memorabilia, and put them together in a unique shape.

Quinceñeras Quilt, Hewlett-Packard Company

Assemble the photos and memorabilia you want to include. Scan or copy your photos and three-dimensional objects. If you have items such as a room key or commemorative pin, you could scan them, print them on fabric, then attach the real objects to your finished quilt.

Consider creating text documents as well; add captions to pictures and identify the meaningful items. Use a fancy—but legible—font and print the documents directly on fabric. Rubber stamps are another option for adding text to a quilt.

Assembling the Quilt

Choose fabrics that will complement your photos. Start putting the pieces together. If you've got it all planned in advance, you can cut the fabrics into the shapes and sizes you need.

Consider making all your fabric photos and scans the same size so it's easier to put them together. Using the largest photo or scan as your guide (and allowing for seams), sew fabric to the top, bottom, and sides of the smaller fabric-printed images until they are all the same size as your largest block. In the *Pet Owner's Quilt* on page 46, one 8" x 10" photo of the dog was used as the center medallion, and all other photos were uniformly cropped and sized.

Once you have a stack of photo blocks, you can cut sashing strips to go between them and start assembling the whole quilt.

If you're creating a scrapbook quilt about a special family vacation, consider putting the photos in chronological order. If it will be a family history quilt, arrange the images with the current family in the center and the ancestors around the edges.

MORE QUICK PROJECTS

1 Design a scrapbook page on paper using your photos and memorabilia. Scan the whole page and print it on fabric for a matching memory album for your quilt. Use the HP Creative Scrapbook Assistant software to make this task a snap.

2 Ask friends to send you photos and handwritten notes for a special birthday or anniversary scrapbook quilt.

3 Use "photo corner" appliqués to make each picture look like it's attached to a scrapbook page. Just cut small triangles from fabric and attach them to each corner.

An easy way to compose your quilt is to place your test prints on a piece of freezer paper or an old bed sheet cut to the approximate final size of your quilt.

Summer Memories

Cyndy Lyle Rymer, Danville, CA, 2003

Finished Quilt Size: 22" x 18½"

Time It Takes to Make: 8–10 hours

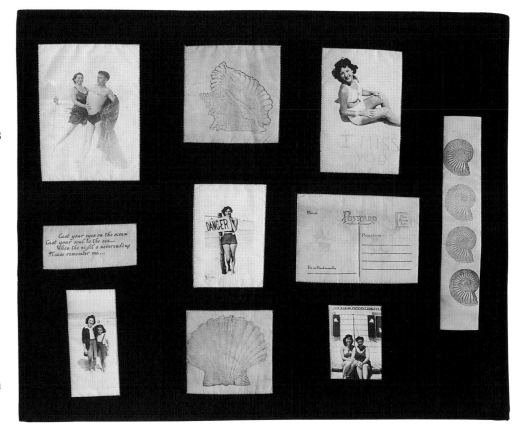

These quilted scrapbook pages were made in a sew-as-you-go style. A family photo album from the 1940s provided some of the photos, as well the basic design idea. The quilt was made without a specific plan in mind. Strips of black fabric were added to every photo, then trimmed as necessary to fit. Rubber stamps that complement the photos provide some fun touches. My grandmother rented the same house for the entire summer for more than 15 years, and three families—including seven cousins—had the most magical times there.

What You Need

- 4–8 pretreated fabric sheets
- 1 yard black for sashing, backing, and binding
- Scraps of muslin for rubber stamps (optional)
- Rubber stamps (optional)
- Fabric ink pads (optional)
- Batting: 24" x 21"
- Large sheet of freezer paper or a design wall

Photo Prep

Scan the photos individually, or gang them on the scanner bed. Print the old black and white photos in color rather than black and white to capture the sepia tint of the photos. Be sure to leave at least ½" of space between the photos for seam allowance.

How to Make the Quilt

1. Play with the photo arrangement on your design wall, or use test prints on freezer paper until you come up with a satisfactory design.

2. Add sashing strips on all sides of each photo and stamped image, if you use stamped "blocks." The key here is to make "blocks" with each photo that can be sewn together to create a 22" x 18" rectangle.

3. Sew the blocks together.

4. Layer and baste the quilt top, batting, and backing.

5. Stitch in-the-ditch around each photo.

6. Bind the quilt.

7. Make a story label to identify your family members, and a made-by label to document your work.

Four Seasons Quilt

Barbara Baker and Jeri Boe,
Bend, OR, 2003

Finished Quilt Size: 34½" x 30½"

Time It Takes to Make:
about 12 hours, plus time
for beading

Celebrate your favorite photos of
the changing seasons, and the
beauty that each has to offer, with
this wallhanging.

What You Need

- 4 pretreated fabric sheets
- Fat quarters of blue, red and yellow for the center and unit squares
- 1 yard green for the sashings and bindings
- ¾ yard black for the background
- 1 yard for the backing
- Batting: 38" x 34"
- Threads to match
- Beads for embellishing (optional)

Photo Prep

Print 2 horizontal 7½" x 10½" photos for Units I and IV, and 2 vertical
7½" x 10½" photos for Units II and III.

How to Make the Quilt

1 Sew 1 green strip 1" x 7½" to each side of Unit I. Press seams to the green.

2 Sew 2 green strips 1" x 11½" to the top and bottom of Unit I. Press seams to the green.

3 Repeat for Unit IV.

4 Sew 1 green strip 1" x 10½" to each side of Unit II. Press seams to the green.

5 Sew 1 green strip 1" x 8½" to the top and bottom of Unit II. Press seams to the green.

6 Repeat for Unit III.

Center Unit

1 Sew 1 black 1½" x 1½" square to 1 blue 1½" x 1½" square. Repeat for black/green and black/red combinations. Press seams to the black.

2 Refer to the quilt diagram and assemble the center unit, adding 1 black 1½" x 1½" square to the right side of the unit. Press seams to the black.

3 Sew 1 black 1½" x 7½" strip to the top and bottom of the center unit. Press seams to the black.

4 Sew 1 green 1" x 3½" strip to each side of the center unit. Press seams to the green.

5 Sew 1 green 1" x 8½" strip to the top and bottom of the center unit. Press to the green. Set aside.

NOTE: There are 2 horizontal pictures for Unit I and IV and 2 vertical pictures for Unit II and III.

Units I–IV

1 Sew 1 blue 2½" x 2½" square to 1 black 2½" x 2½" square. Repeat for green/black combination. Press to the black.

2 Sew 1 red 2½" x 2½" square to 1 black 1½" x 2½" strip. Press to the black.

3 Sew blue/black, green/black, and red/black units into a strip. Follow the photo on page 51 and quilt diagram at right to complete the other 3 checkerboard strips.

4 Follow the quilt diagram to sew Unit I together using the checkerboard unit, photo, 1 black 2½" x 11½" strip, and 1 black 3½" x 11½" strip. Repeat for Unit IV.

5 Sew Unit II together using the checkerboard unit, photo, 1 black 1½" x 11½" strip, 1 black 3½" x 11½" strip, and 1 black 5½" x 11½" strip. Repeat for Unit III.

Partial Seam

1 Refer to the Quilt Assembly Diagram for the correct placement. Sew the center unit to Unit III, starting the seam ¼" from the beginning of the center unit. This will be sewn in the final seam.

2 Sew this unit to Unit IV. Press seam open.

3 Sew this unit to Unit II. Press seam open.

4 Sew this unit to Unit I. Press seam open.

5 Now complete the partial seam for Unit III. Press the seam open.

Borders

1 Sew 1 black strip 2½" x 26½" to each side of the quilt top. Press seams to the border.

2 Sew 1 black strip 2½" x 34½" to the top and bottom of the quilt top. Press seams to the border.

3 Layer your quilt top with the batting and backing. Pin or thread-baste the layers together.

4 Quilt in the pictures following the designs in the picture. Quilt the rest of the quilt as desired.

5 Bind.

Quilt Assembly Diagram. All sizes unfinished measurements.

2½" x 11½"

Unit I

3½" x 11½"

3½" x 11½"

Unit II

5½" x 11½"

1½" x 11½"

Center unit

Begin sewing here.

3½" x 11½"

1½" x 11½"

5½" x 11½"

Unit III

3½" x 11½"

Unit IV

2½" x 11½"

Travel Memories Quilt

Lynn Koolish, Berkeley, CA, 2001

Finished Quilt Size: 14" x 44"

Time It Takes to Make:
about 10 hours

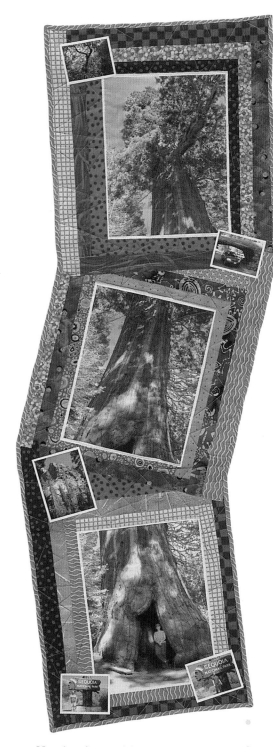

What You Need

- 4 pretreated fabric sheets
- 1½ yards fusible web
- Fabric scraps for strips
- Base fabric: 1 yard
- Binding: ¼ yard
- Optional: Teflon pressing sheet (placed over the photos and scraps while fusing; protects your iron)

Photo Prep

Print the photos as 8" x 10" photos, or use your scanner to enlarge and crop the photo, then print.

How to Make the Quilt

1 Cut the photos and scraps slightly larger than needed. Back the photos and scraps of fabric with fusible web to the edge of the pieces, following the manufacturer's instructions.

2 Cut 1 rectangle to the desired size of the base fabric.

3 Arrange the photos on the base. Trim photos to size, then fuse to the base fabric following the manufacturer's instructions.

4 Trim the strips to the desired size, and place around the photos in a Log Cabin pattern. For example, fuse a strip to the right side of the photo. Add strips in a clockwise fashion around the bottom, left, and top of the photo.

5 Trim the base to the desired shape and size.

6 Layer the quilt top, batting, and backing.

7 Quilt as desired. Lynn quilted the tree trunks and branches, and random straight-stitch quilted the outer sections of the blocks.

8 Bind.

Here's a fast and fun machine appliqué quilt made with a series of favorite vacation photos. The center photos were fused to a backing fabric, and strips of fabric backed with fusible web were added around the photos in a freestyle Log Cabin pattern. Smaller photos were fused in strategic spots to add even more visual interest.

Windowpane Quilt

Summertime Fun, Hewlett-Packard Company

Posterize It!

Windowpane quilts are wonderful vehicles for enlarging a favorite photo to poster size, and an easy way to make a great gift. Use the technique of your choice described on pages 56–57. The sections are printed as separate quilt blocks, then sewn back together with or without sashing strips.

All you need is a scanned or digital image, an inkjet printer, some pretreated fabric sheets, sewing supplies, and your imagination. Best of all, you don't need elaborate photo-editing software. Any basic software with photo-editing capability that allows you to crop or resize images will work just fine.

Now more than ever it's very important to make test prints on paper.

GOOD to KNOW

1 The final quality of the photo prints depends on the photo used. Digital prints work the best because you are printing from an original, not from a copy. If you are using a standard printed photo, it's best to start with an enlarged photo, such as an 8" x 10".

2 Resolution counts when you scan a digitized photo. The higher the resolution of your original digital photo, the more you can enlarge it without losing image resolution. (See Just What Is Resolution Anyway? on page 20.)

3 Plan for seamlines when you divide your photos. You don't want the seamlines to end up in the center of someone's face.

4 Use photo image-editing software that offers a ruler and grid option to resize the photo sections. This makes it much easier to ensure that the proportions of the original photo are maintained.

5 Resized photo sections should be no larger than 8" x 10" to allow a ¼" seam allowance on all sides.

6 Under Options, select "Best" for the Print Quality and "Plain" for the Paper Type before printing.

What You Need

- Your favorite digital image or scanned photo
- 4 or more 8½" x 11" pretreated inkjet printer fabric sheets
- Inkjet printer
- Scissors, or rotary cutter, ruler, and cutting mat
- Image-editing software such as Photoshop Elements
- Fabrics to complement the photo
- Batting

Ways to Divide Your Picture

Before you can print out the pieces of your windowpane picture quilt, you'll need to enlarge your photo and divide it into sections. The easiest way is to use the HP poster printing feature. If that function is unavailable on your inkjet printer, either of the other methods will produce the same great results with a little extra effort.

1. Use the Poster Printing Option

By using the poster printing option included with your HP inkjet printer, your digital photo is automatically enlarged and divided into fabric sheets. For example, if you select 3 x 3 (3 sheets across and 3 sheets down), your photo is automatically enlarged and divided to fit on 9 fabric sheets (3 sheets across and 3 sheets down).

- Open the photo in your software application.
- Use the software tools to enlarge the photo to approximately 8" x 10".
- Select "Print" from the File menu.
- Click the "Properties" button.
- Click the "Poster Printing" box on the "Features" tab.
- Select the poster printing size option that you want: 2 x 2, 3 x 3, or 4 x 4.
- Click OK.

2. Use Image-Editing Software

- Open the photo in the software application of your choice.
- Use software image-editing tools to divide your digital image.
- Using the editing tools available with the software, divide the photo into sections on the screen. The number of sections corresponds to the number of fabric sheets you'll need. For example, if you divide the photo into 4 sections, you'll need 4 fabric sheets to print out the photo.
- Place each photo section in a separate document so each will print out on a separate sheet.
- Enlarge each divided section by exactly the same percentage, but to no more than 8" x 10". You will need the extra space around the edge of each sheet for the seam allowance when you sew the sections together.

3. Cut It Up and Scan It

Cut your photo (or a good quality copy of it) apart, then scan the individual pieces as separate graphics files. Make a copy of the photo before starting.

- Divide and cut your photo into the number of sections you need to make the size of picture quilt you want. For example, if you use 4 photos 8" x 10" each, your quilt will be at least 22" wide with the addition of 1" sashing strips between the photos, and with 2" borders.

- Scan and save each section as a separate graphic file.

- Open the graphics inside the software application of your choice.

- Place each graphic on a separate page.

- Enlarge each divided section by exactly the same percentage, but to no more than 8" x 10". You will need the extra space around the edge of each sheet for the seam allowance when you sew the sections together.

Printing

- Load a fabric sheet into the printer. Insert only one fabric sheet into the printer at a time.

- Print all the fabric sheets.

- After printing, remove the backing from the fabric sheet and allow to dry according to the manufacturer's directions.

Sewing

1 Trim approximately ½" (or half the finished width of your sashing strips) on all sides of each photo section to account for the portion of the picture that would not be seen if it were behind an actual windowpane sash.

2 Sew the sashing strips, then the borders, to the fabric photos.

3 Layer the quilt top, batting, and backing. Trim the quilt to the desired size and shape. Quilt as desired.

4 Bind the quilt.

5 Add a customized label on the back with a smaller version of the original photo.

Best Friends, Hewlett-Packard Company

Record the Story

Using the HP Custom Quilt Label Kit

You've invested a lot of time, energy, and love into making your quilt; maybe it's a gift, or intended to celebrate a special occasion. Each quilt you make has a story to tell. Without a label, the quilt's story might be lost someday.

The easy-to-use HP Custom Quilt Label Kit helps you create unique, professional labels to document your quilt. It offers you the choice of templates or creating your own layout for story labels and "made by" labels in a matter of minutes. Use your own photos and artwork, or choose from hundreds of included images and clip art. The kit also includes a collection of thoughtful sentiments and quilting phrases.

You can use the kit to create a matching gift card to accompany your quilt. The kit also offers the ability to create smaller "made by" labels, with room for your name, the date, the occasion, and a small piece of artwork. Learn more about it at www.hp.com/go/quilting/book.

Story Labels

A story label is bigger than a traditional label. There is plenty of room in this format to note the recipient's and maker's names, the date and occasion, and important details about the quilt, with space for photos or clip art. Name the quilt pattern, or tell a story about making the quilt. You could also make a story label for an antique quilt whose history you've researched.

QUICK LABEL IDEAS

The name of the quilt and the pattern, and when it will be given and to whom

1 The special occasion for which the quilt is given and to whom

2 How long it took to make, and any noteworthy facts about its construction

3 Photographs, artwork, and memorabilia

4 Any special meaning behind the fabric selection

5 A verse or quotation—one you've written or one you find that fits the sentiment behind the quilt

6 Include a photograph of yourself. Your greatgrandchildren may never meet you, but if the quilt label includes your photo, they'll always be able to remember you.

It's simple to use a pre-made template:

1 Open the design, and change the text or other items (like a background color or photo) if you wish.

2 Print on a fabric sheet.

You can also start with a blank template. The kit includes a selection of borders and backgrounds, and you can add digital photos or a scanned image of the quilt fabric to create a one-of-a-kind border or background.

Top Tips and Tricks

Explore the HP Custom Quilt Label Kit's features to further personalize your quilt labels and gift cards. As you do, you may discover some of your own favorite tips and tricks.

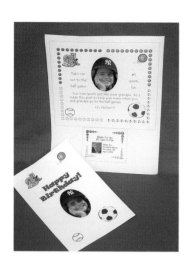

1 Use your own images as borders and backgrounds to make your quilt label or gift card even more meaningful, such as a colorful border made from a photo of pansies, or a scenic photo from a family vacation.

2 Use digital photos of completed quilts as images, borders, or backgrounds. You can add borders to any placeholder within a label or gift card—not just around the edges.

3 Layer borders and backgrounds to create unique frames. Layering just a couple of borders and backgrounds creates interesting effects. It's a good idea to keep the number of layers to a minimum to keep the file size small when you save the label or gift card.

4 Create a palette of colors that matches your quilt perfectly. The color controls for borders, backgrounds, and text show a small collection of colors in a pop-up window for quick and easy access. You can also use the "more colors" option on the color palette to choose a larger color chart and build your custom color palette.

5 Add text boxes for a mix of different fonts, font sizes, styles, and colors. The Add Text button lets you create new text boxes anywhere in your label or gift card. You can also change the size or appearance of text boxes.

6 Add a splash of color by experimenting with the Text Background and Text Color features. For example, try white text on a dark blue background.

7 To make sure your label design allows room for a ¼" seam allowance along each side, turn on the Seam Allowance feature. You'll see a dashed line both on-screen and when you print your label, to indicate the fold line.

Ode to Speck, Joe Hesch and Sue Anderson

8 When you insert an image into a placeholder, the image may not fill the entire placeholder on all sides. You can instantly fill the space with a background color or add a border from the Solid Border/Background Color palette.

9 You can quickly access the HP Quilting website from the Help menu by selecting HP Quilt Community Web Site. You'll find tips on getting pictures onto your computer, printing on fabric, and more. See www.hp.com/go/quilting/book.

10 Maximize space on a fabric sheet by creating custom-sized labels. Using the blank templates from the New dialog box, you can create a label of any size up to a full page. Create several smaller labels, sizing their elements as you like, and print them on one fabric sheet. The kit includes templates for coordinated sets of Story labels and Made-By labels, which also maximize the space on a fabric sheet.

11 Take advantage of the many ready-made designs in the kit. Use one as your base design and personalize it with your own images and text. With very little time or effort, you'll see professional-quality results. Don't worry about overwriting a ready-made design after you've modified it; you'll be asked for a new file name when you save your design.

Beyond Quilt Labels

Like many quilters, you'll soon discover that the HP Custom Quilt Label Kit can create more than just labels.

1 Make appliqués with the high-quality images or clip art from the kit. Drag an image into a blank template, enlarge or reduce the image's size, print it on a printable fabric sheet, cut it out, and then sew it onto your quilt. (Even faster, print the appliqué on fusible fabric and iron it on.)

2 Use artwork and background images from the kit to create quilted animals that will delight the children in your life.

3 Try using images, clip art, or backgrounds from the kit or your own images as primary blocks in your quilt. Enlarge an image or piece of clip art to fill a blank template, or simply flood the template with a background. Print and use as you would any fabric.

4 Print one-of-a-kind fabric labels tailored to each child's interests and personality. Use the kit's Made-By label template, or use a blank template to design your own. Add the child's photo or a favorite image (like a train or ballerina), name, and any other details.

5 Add a quilter's touch to any ordinary framed photo. Use a blank template to create a border or a colorful background. Add a poem or description of the photo, and print it on plain paper or printable fabric sheets. Place the photo beneath the border or on top of the background with some of the background showing around the edges. Frame it for a one-of-a-kind work of art.

6 Create a brief bio to include with any quilts you give as gifts or share with fellow quilters. Use a blank landscape or portrait Story label or Made-By label template, add a colorful border or background with photos of yourself and your favorite quilts.

7 Create personalized aprons, tote bags, lunch bags, pillowcases, garment bags and more. Just use a blank template and add photos, artwork, and text. Then print it on printable fabric sheets.

8 Need a gift card for your next special occasion? The HP Custom Quilt Label Kit includes a wide variety of artwork and a large collection of themed phrases to choose from. Consider making a quilted gift card.

9 Give one of your quilts star treatment on the card front. Print the back of your quilt on the other side of the card.

10 For your next party, use the artwork, borders, and backgrounds in the HP Custom Quilt Label Kit to create coordinated invitations, name tags, and name cards for place settings.

Half Dome, Sandy Hart, Los Gatos, CA. From the collection of Angie Hart.

Resources

HEWLETT-PACKARD COMPANY
www.hp.com/go/quilting/book

CARYL BRYER FALLERT
Bryerpatch Studio www.bryerpatch.com

COLOR TEXTILES
9030 West Sahara
Box 198
Las Vegas, NV 89117
www.colortextiles.com
Pretreated fabric sheets include: poplin,
cotton broadcloth, silk, white denim, linen,
silk chiffon, silk crepe de chine

MILLIKEN & COMPANY
Spartanburg, SC
www.milliken.com
email: info@printedtreasures.com
Printed Treasures pretreated cotton
fabric sheets

JUNE TAILOR
P.O. Box 208
2861 Highway 175
Richfield WI 53076
800-844-5400
www.junetailor.com
Cream and white pretreated cotton
fabric sheets

MOUNTAIN MIST
The Stearns Technical Textiles Company
2551 Crescentville Rd.
Cincinnati OH 45215
800-345-7150
www.stearntextiles.com
Mountain Mist Print-Fab Iron-on stabilizer;
use instead of freezer paper—reusable!

C. JENKINS NECKTIE & CHEMICAL COMPANY
39 S. Schlueter
Dellwood, MO 63135
314-521-7544
www.cjenkinscompany.com
Bubble Jet Set 2000 ink fixative,
freezer paper sheets, pretreated fabric rolls

SCRAP SMART
180 Metro Park
Rochester NY 14623
800-424-1011
www.ScrapSmart.com
Scrapbook covers, scrapbook pages

DOVER PUBLICATIONS
31 East 2nd Street
Mineola, NY 11501-3582
Fax: 516-294-9758
www.doverpublications.com
Great source for CD/book sets of permission-
free photos and clip art

Books

Astroth, Sue, **Fast, Fun & Easy Scrapbook
Quilts**, Lafayette, CA: C&T Publishing, 2004.

Laury, Jean Ray, **Imagery on Fabric, 2nd ed.**,
Lafayette, CA: C&T Publishing, 1997.

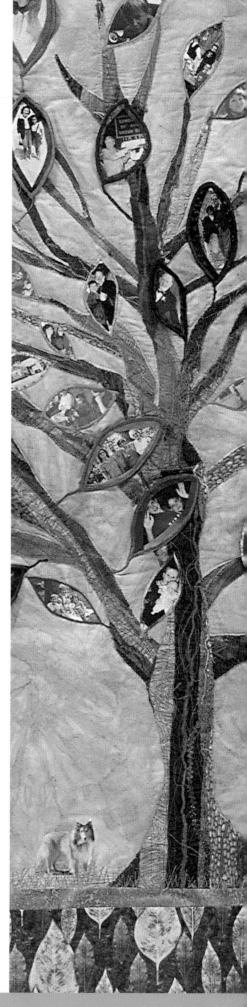

Underwater Ivy,
15" x 12",
Karyn Hoyt-Culp,
Alameda, CA, 2003.
Original photo used
with permission of
Tue Nam Ton.

Meet the HP Quilting Team

Hewlett Packard is a world leader in printing and imaging and has dedicated an entire team to help quilters enjoy using technology products in their craft. By providing hardware and software solutions designed by quilters for quilters, HP is helping make this exciting new aspect of quilting come to life. No worries, no complicated instructions or hard to understand technology, HP's offerings of cameras, printers, scanners, software and quilting website all make it easy. More than ever, it is fun and exciting to capture memories and express yourself in quilting adding that special, personalized touch. Visit HP's quilting website for all the latest projects, tips and inspiration at www.hp.com/go/quilting/book But first, let's meet the team...

Pictured from left to right: Shauna Beatty, Sandra Zatta, Marie Hemberry, Steve Dentel, Deb Jungkind, Joe Hesch

An introduction to our team:
Deb Jungkind: Quilting program manager, webmaster, and all-around queen bee.
Joe Hesch: Customer education manager, technical director of this book, and quilter
Steve Haines (not pictured) and Shauna Beatty: Marketing extraordinaires (aka trouble-makers).
Steve Dentel: Software development guru
Sandra Zatta: Trade show coordinator and problem fixer
Marie Hemberry: Customer support, staff support, project support, you get it...

Special thanks to: Sue Anderson, Curiosity Group Inc., Kathleen Brown, Craig Hamer, Sue Hausmann and the VSM staff, Lori Dvir-Djerassi, Hugh Amick, Hazel Price, Jon Firooz, Cory Carpenter, Loverink documentation services, and the very professional C&T Publishing staff: Amy Marson, Jan Grigsby, and Cyndy Lyle Rymer.

Cyndy Lyle Rymer is a development editor at C&T Publishing. Before quilting, her first passion was photography. The chance to work on this book was an opportunity to make the leap into the new technology available to quilters. One quilt definitely leads to another, and another, and...

Index